Winter W

Charles Ellingworth

These are some things I have enjoyed, or found interesting, over the last year.

I hope you feel the same.

Copyright © 2023 Charles Ellingworth

ISBN: 9798870055633

PublishNation
www.publishnation.co.uk

It is an astonishment to be alive, and it behoves you to be astonished.
John Donne

Egoist: a person low taste – more interested in himself than me.
Ambrose Pierce: The Devil's Dictionary

There is no such thing as fun for the whole family.
Jerry Seinfeld

Tolerance will reach such a level that intelligent people will be banned from thinking so as not to offend the imbeciles.
Dostoyevsky

Although written many years ago, Lady Chatterley's Lover has just been reissued by the Grove Press, and this fictional account of the day-to-day life of an English gamekeeper is still of considerable interest to outdoor minded readers, as it contains many passages on pheasant raising, the apprehending of poachers, ways to control vermin, and other chores and duties of the professional gamekeeper. Unfortunately, one is obliged to wade through many pages of extraneous material in order to discover and savour these sidelights on the management of a Midlands shooting estate, and in this reviewer's opinion this book cannot take the place of J.R. Miller's Practical Gamekeeping
A review of Lady Chatterley's Lover in Field and Stream, November 1959

The history of our race, and each individual's experience, are sown thick with evidence that a truth is not hard to kill and that a lie told well is immortal.
Mark Twain

Don't worry about people stealing your ideas. If your ideas are any good, you'll have to ram them down people's throats.
Howard Aiken

There was never a good war, or a bad peace.
Benjamin Franklin

There are some experiences in life which should not be demanded twice from any man, and one of them is listening to the Brahms Requiem.
George Bernard Shaw

Music is entirely independent of the phenomenal world, ignores it altogether, could to a certain extent exist if there was no world at all. This is why the effect of music is so much more powerful and penetrating than that of the other arts, for they speak only of shadows, but music speaks of the thing itself.
Schopenhauer

There's only a razor's edge between self-confidence and hubris.
Jack Welch

A simple rule in dealing with those who are hard to get along with is to remember that this person is striving to assert his superiority; and you must deal with him from that point of view.
Alfred Adler

When people are free to do as they please, they usually imitate each other.
Eric Hoffer

On this earth, in the final analysis, each of us gets exactly what he deserves. But only the successful recognize this.
Georges Simenon

There have been as many plagues as wars in history; yet always wars and plagues take people equally by surprise.
Albert Camus, The Plague

You don't have to deserve your mother's love. You have to deserve your father's. He's more particular.
Robert Frost

He who wishes to be rich in a day will be hanged in a year.
Leonardo da Vinci

There is a special type of middle-class snob that doesn't like to see working-class people in designer labels — they'll use the word vulgar, or showy, or blingy, or that most hateful of terms, chav. They like sneering at football WAGs, with their Louis Vuitton bags and Louboutin heels. They prefer working-class people who can be described as "proud" or "down to earth"; ie, happy with their lot. Easy to say, when the lot is not yours. This disdain has always been curious to me and I sometimes wonder whether it's because a taste for the fancier things is taken as a rejection of the middle-class way of life. An aspirational working-class person is not trying to become middle class, even if this is where they/we end up. No one grows up on a council estate dreaming of Boden and Riverford organic veg boxes.
Lesley Thomas

Merry Christmas to EVERYONE, including the Radical Left Marxists that are trying to destroy our Country, the Federal Bureau of Investigation that is illegally coercing & paying Social and LameStream Media to push for a mentally disabled Democrat over the Brilliant, Clairvoyant, and USA LOVING Donald J. Trump.
The Trump Christmas message 2022

I am not sure what you are talking about. I get up in the morning. I do the best I can all day. I go to bed in the evening, say my prayers and go to sleep. What do you do?
The late Queen - when asked whether she lay awake worrying.

The cleverly expressed opposite of any generally accepted idea is worth a fortune to somebody.
F. Scott Fitzgerald

The joys of parents are secret, and so are their griefs and fears.
Sir Francis Bacon

The stillness that became William Hurt's trademark on screen was somewhat in contrast to a manic personality off camera. He suffered from logorrhoea, or excessive talkativeness, which he treated with lithium, and interviews with him sometimes read like a script from one of Dr Anthony Clare's In the Psychiatrist's Chair programmes.
 One interviewer reported that when asked how shooting on his latest film was going, Hurt answered with "a thesis on the interconnectedness of quantum mechanics, Tibetan Buddhism, infected blood, the Gulf War, chaos theory and third world population growth". Another question prompted references to William Blake and Spinoza. It wasn't pomposity, simply the way that his overactive mind worked. His first wife noted with evident frustration that "most people will just eat a hamburger; he will want to know where the cow was born".
From the Times Obituary of William Hurt

Dear Sir,
Professor Lovell calculates in The Sunday Times this morning that there must be at least 1,000 other planets in this universe equally as far developed as our own, but one thing I am certain of is that on all these planets there cannot be a single broadcaster with an equally pansy bastard strangulated voice like yours.
Bamber Gascoigne's first 'fan letter'

The funniest joke about democracy is that it gives its enemies the means to destroy it.
Joseph Goebbels

People are always shouting that they want to create a better future. It's not true. The future is an apathetic void of no interest to anyone. The past is full of life, eager to irritate us, provoke us and insult us, tempt us to destroy or repaint it. The only reason people want to be masters of the future is to change the past.
Milan Kundera

"We're retired now, but in our spare time we like to choose the next prime minister"

These are actors,
As I fortold you, were all spirits, and
Are melted into air, into thin air;
And, like the baseless fabric of this vision,
the cloud-capp'd towers, the gorgeous palaces,
The solemn temples, the great globe itself,
Aye all which it inherit, shall dissolve
And, like this insubstantial pageant faded,
Leave not a rack behind. We are such stuff.
as dreams are made on, and our little life
is rounded with a sleep.
The Tempest

Every new beginning comes from some other beginning's end.
Seneca the Elder

Suppose you were an idiot. And suppose you were a member of Congress. But I repeat myself.
Mark Twain

The despair I can handle; it's the hope I can't bear.
John Cleese in Clockwork

Murphy's Law: What can go wrong will go wrong.
Sod's Corollary: Murphy was an optimist.

It is frequently a misfortune to have very brilliant men in charge of affairs. They expect too much of ordinary men.
Thucydides

Fox News has done to our parents' brains what they said video games would do to ours.
An anonymous millennial

Feeling resentment is like drinking poison and waiting for the other person to die.
St Augustine

It's not about how old you are, it's about how you are old. Don't anybody ever retire! Do not embrace old age! It's crap! I haven't got time for that rubbish.
Brian Blessed

This is from Akenfield by Ronald Bythe - who died this year; a portrait of a village in Suffolk in the mid 20th Century. Many modern metropolitans romanticise the country lives of the past - which were, in reality, brutally hard.

Len is also an extraordinarily interesting survivor of Britain's village lost generation, of that mysterious army of horsemen, ploughmen and field workers who fled the wretchedness of the farms in 1914. The army had provided – along with the railways – an escape route for many years before this, but it was the First World War which swept Len and his contemporaries off the hated land to conditions which forced the thinking countryman to decide to halt a system of degradation when they returned. The climate of the 1920s and 1930s suited Len perfectly for what he had to do. The war had given those who survived it confidence. Len showed his by stolidly denying the village farmers their virtual ownership of the labourers and their families. He organized the union branch. The successes and defeats of the struggle, which was basically a nineteenth-century one and little different from that of Joseph Arch and his colleagues, suited him excellently. He wanted 'improvement', not metamorphosis. But for a man of Len's age, the change which has swept through the village is metamorphosis, neither more nor less, and so one sees him, a fine old man, doing his utmost to comprehend the foreign place in which he happened to have been born. Grandchildren arrive during the university holidays. Nephews and nieces fly in from Canada, while the ash at the end of the road, which marked the last point at which soldier and emigrant sons could turn and wave before walking to Ipswich to catch the train to Gallipoli or Quebec, still blocks the view.

When you adopt the standards and the values of someone else you surrender your own integrity. You become, to the extent of your surrender, less of a human being.
Eleanor Roosevelt

To have doubted one's own first principles is the mark of a civilized man.
Oliver Wendell Holmes

A great many people think they are thinking when they are merely rearranging their prejudices.
William James

Man is the creature of the era he lives in; very few can raise themselves above the ideas of the time.
Voltaire

Truth is what your contemporaries let you get away with saying.
Richard Rorty

Formerly known as Prince

I long for the day of judgement, when the plot lines of our lives will be neatly tied and all puzzles, explained and the meaning of events made clear. We take to fiction, I suppose, because no such thing is going to happen.
Fay Weldon

Our earth is degenerate in these latter days: bribery and corruption are common; children no longer obey their parents; every man wants to write a book, and the end of the world is evidently approaching.
Inscription on an Assyrian Tablet

I caught this morning morning's minion, kingdom of daylight's dauphin, dapple-dawn-drawn Falcon, in his riding

Of the rolling level underneath him steady air, and striding
High there, how he rung upon the rein of a wimpling wing
In his ecstasy! then off, off forth on swing,
As a skate's heel sweeps smooth on a bow-bend: the hurl and gliding
Rebuffed the big wind. My heart in hiding
Stirred for a bird, — the achieve of, the mastery of the thing!
Gerard Manley Hopkins: The Windhover

Death makes a mockery of almost everything else we spend most of our lives doing. Just take a moment to reflect on how you spent your day so far. The kind of things that captured your attention, the things that you've been genuinely worried about... Contemplating the brevity of life brings some perspective to how we use our attention. It's not so much what we pay attention to – it's the quality of the attention. It's how we feel while doing it. If you need to spend the next hour looking for something, you might as well enjoy it. Because the truth is that none of us know how much time we have in this life and taking that fact to heart brings a kind of moral and emotional clarity to the present. And it can bring a resolve not to suffer over stupid things.

Take something like road rage: you're behind the wheel of your car, and somebody does something erratic, or probably just driving more slowly than you want, and you find yourself getting angry. Now I would submit to you that that kind of thing is impossible if you're being mindful of the shortness of life. If you're aware that you're going to die, and that the other person is going to die, and that you're both going to lose everyone you love, and that you don't know when, you've got this moment of life, this beautiful moment, this moment when your consciousness is bright, when it's not dimmed by morphine in hospital on your last day amongst the living. And the sun is out, or it's raining, both are beautiful, and your spouse is alive, and your children are alive, and you're driving.

And that person in front of you, who you will never meet – whose hopes and sorrows, you know nothing about, but if you could know them, you would recognise are impressively similar to your own – is just driving slowly.

This is your life: the only one you've got. And you'll never get this moment back again. And you don't know how many more moments you have. No matter how many times you do something, there will come a time when you do it for the last time. You've had a thousand chances to tell the people closest to you that you love them in a way that they feel it and in a way that you feel it, and you've missed most of them, and you don't know how many more you're going to get.

You've got this next interaction with another human being to make the world a marginally better place. You've got this one opportunity to fall in love with existence. So why not relax and enjoy your life? Really relax, even in the midst of struggle, even under uncertainty. You are in a game right now, and you can't see the clock, so you don't know how much time you have left. And yet you're free to make the game as interesting as possible. You can even change the rules: you can discover new games that no one has thought of yet. But whatever you do, however seemingly ordinary, you can feel the preciousness of life. And an awareness of death is the doorway into that way of being in the world.

Sam Harris: The Lessons of Death

When I was a boy of fourteen, my father was so ignorant I could hardly stand to have the old man around. But when I got to be twenty-one, I was astonished by how much he'd learned in seven years.

Mark Twain

The first one-pound note was issued in 1797 by the Bank of England, although the curious-looking £ symbol had already been around for some time to designate a pound sterling. The Bank of England Museum holds a cheque dated 7 January 1661, in which the sign is clearly visible.

The symbol is a representation of the letter L, with one or two crossbars added to indicate an abbreviation. The L itself stood for the Latin word libra, meaning 'scales' or 'balance' - hence the traditional icon of the star sign Libra, and a Roman unit of weight. It was generally written as libra pondo - in which pondo , the ancestor of the English 'pound ', meant 'by weight'.

Libra also gave us the abbreviation 'lb', for a pound in weight. A pound sterling originally had the value of a pound weight of sterling silver - 'sterling' having got its name from early Norman coins that were adorned with little stars.

The pound note was withdrawn from circulation in England in 1988, and replaced by a coin that bore around its patterned, grooved edge the inscription 'decus et tutamen', taken from Virgil's Aeneid, meaning 'adornment and protection'. The phrase was originally inscribed on a shield presented to a victorious warrior; it was chosen as an inscription by the Bank of England because the motto was both an embellishment and a safeguard - in the days when coins were made of precious metal, coin-clipping, whereby coins were filed down, was a serious threat. Today's twelve-sided design is intended to be even harder to counterfeit.
Suzie Dent: Word Perfect

The wicked have only accomplices; voluptuaries have companions in debauch, self-seekers have partners, politicians attract partisans; the generality of idle men have attachments; princes have courtiers, and virtuous men alone have friends.
Voltaire

Civilisation and anarchy are only seven meals apart.
Spanish Proverb

If there were no bad people, there would be no good lawyers.
Dickens

Choice of attention - to pay attention to this and ignore that - is to the inner life what choice of action is to the outer. In both cases, a man is responsible for his choice and must accept the consequences.
W.H. Auden

There is nothing as easy as denouncing. It don't take much to see that something is wrong, but it takes some eyesight to see what will put it right again.
Will Rogers

The view that the rate of interest is determined by 'real' economic, as opposed to monetary, factors was advanced by the Scottish philosopher David Hume in his influential essay 'Of Interest' (1752). Yet Hume's claim that interest rates are unaffected by changes in the money supply is not supported by the ancient history. After Alexander the Great seized and distributed large stocks of Persian gold and silver, prices are said to have risen and interest rates declined. Suetonius, in The Twelve Caesars, describes how, when the Emperor Augustus brought the treasure belonging to the kings of Egypt back to Rome, money became plentiful and interest rates fell from 6 to 4 per cent. After Augustus' death, the Emperor Tiberius hoarded money, with the result that interest rates rose above the legal limit and a banking crisis erupted in AD 33. Tiberius then decided to lend out the imperial treasure free of interest to patrician families, which brought about an immediate decline in interest rates and an end to the crisis. His actions constituted the world's first experience of quantitative easing.
Edward Chancellor: The Price of Time

My definition of an intellectual is someone who can listen to the William Tell Overture without thinking of the Lone Ranger.
Billy Connolly

The former astronaut Buzz Aldrin was flooded with congratulatory messages when he marked his 93rd birthday last month by marrying for the fourth time. But none came from Jeremy Clarkson. "I've always never wanted to meet him because he's famously difficult' Clarkson wrote in The Sun. "A few years ago, he agreed to take part in a live interview, and as the director used his fingers to count down silently from five, he leaned over to the reporter and, with one second to go, said: 'Nothing about the Moon, OK?'"
From The Week

It is not true that suffering ennobles the character; happiness does that sometimes, but suffering, for the most part, makes men petty and vindictive.
Somerset Maughan

Men are more easily governed through their vices than through their virtues.
Napoleon

This is a letter from Manuela Seanz, the long-time lover of Simon Bolivar, to her much older English husband. She was quite a woman - and called Libertadora del libertador" (liberator of the liberator) by Bolivar after she saved his life twice - once from an assassination attempt.

No, no, no, hombre... A thousand times No! Sir, you are an excellent person, indeed one of a kind—that I will never deny. I only regret that you are not a better man so that my leaving you would honour Bolivar more. I know very well that I can never be joined to him in what you call honour. Do you think I am any less honourable because he is my lover, not my husband? Ah! I do not live by social conventions men construct to torment us. So leave me be, my dear Englishman, We will marry again in heaven but not on this earth.... On earth, you are a boring man. Up there in the celestial heights, everything will be so English, because a life of monotony was invented for you people, who make love without pleasure, conversation without grace—who walk slowly, greet solemnly, move heavily, and joke without laughing.... but enough of my cheekiness. With all the sobriety, truth, and clarity of an Englishwoman, I say now: I will never return to you. you are a Protestant, and I am a pagan, - that should be obstacle enough, but I am also in love with another man, and that is the greater and stronger reason. You see how precise my mind can be.
Your invariable friend,
Manuela

Man only likes to count his troubles, but he does not count his joys.
Dostoevsky

No man ever listened himself out of a job.
Calvin Coolidge

The collegiate structure of oratorian life suited Dilke. Initially he was known as Father Sebastian, as the community already had a Father Charles, whose real name was Michael. When an oratorian named Father Michael left. Father Charles resumed the name Michael, allowing Sebastian to become Father Charles.
From the Times obituary of Rev Sir Charles Dilke Bt, a catholic priest at the London Oratory for 56 years

We can easily forgive a child who is afraid of the dark; the real tragedy of life is when men are afraid of the light.
Plato

At the end of the war if there are two Americans and one Russian left, we win.
General Thomas Power, C-in-C of Strategic Air Command during the Cuban Missile Crisis. With military stupidity on this scale, it's amazing that we are still here.

The lasting legacy of Kievan Rus was in religion and the cultural sphere, where Byzantium would permanently mark Russian civilisation. Some of the fundamental ideas that would shape the course of Russian history – the idea of Holy Rus, the

sacred status of the monarchy, the principle of oligarchic power – can be traced back to the Byzantine inheritance. But it is absurd to claim that Kievan Rus was the birthplace of the modern Russian or Ukrainian state. Perhaps, in the end, we should look at Kievan Rus as part of Russia's 'ancient history' – a period related to its later history in the same sense as Anglo-Saxon Wessex is part of English history or Merovingian Gaul is linked to modern France – namely as a source of the country's religion, its language and its artistic forms. The rest of the Kievan heritage in Russia has been lost.
Orlando Figes: The Story of Russia. Sorry Putin.

Humility is the real key to the Christian virtues, for without it we keep all our faults which pride merely conceals from others and often from ourselves.
de La Rochefoucauld

The nearest Raquel Welch came to a celebrity wedding was not as a bride but as the mother of the groom when Damon (her son) married Rebecca Trueman, the daughter of Freddie Trueman, the Yorkshire and England cricketer and self-proclaimed "finest fast bowler that ever drew breath". At the blessing ceremony in the Yorkshire Dales, she upset the Trueman family by upstaging the bride with her revealing dress and flamboyant late entrance with a posse of bodyguards. Trueman's mother Ethel told her she looked like a trollop and Enid, the cricketer's ex-wife, complained that Welch had "ruined" her daughter's wedding. "Her boobs were showing and her skirt was up her bum," she said. Trueman was less censorious and described her as "a little smasher".
The couple separated 15 months later when Rebecca walked out of their plush Los Angeles apartment and returned to Yorkshire. "It did not last as long as one of my run-ups," Trueman noted laconically.
She recounted with a deliciously deadpan humour how the iconic bikini image came about as they were shooting against the volcanic backdrop of Lanzarote. "You see that rock over there? That's rock A. When I call action, you start running to rock B, which is over there," the director Don Chaffey told her.

"When you get halfway between the two, pretend you see a giant turtle coming at you, and you scream. Then we break for lunch. Got it?"
It was winter and the entire cast and crew apart from the shivering Welch were dressed in parkas. She went down with a severe case of tonsillitis.
From Raquel Welch's Obituary in The Times

The trouble with the Engenglish is that their hiss hiss history happened overseas, so they dodo don't know what it means.
Whisky Sisodia in Salman Rushdie's The Satanic Verses

The love in your heart wasn't put there to stay. Love isn't love 'til you give it away.
Oscar Hammerstein

Balance isn't particularly useful thing in history. You wouldn't ask an historian to list the pros and cons of Adolf Hitler. Nuance is everything.
Sathnam Sanghera

Life is a tragedy for those who feel, and a comedy for those who think.
La Bruyere. I'm still trying to work out what I think about this....

This is from a review in the Literary Review by Alberto Manguel of Ítalo Calvino's The Written World and the Unwritten World.

And yet there is a page that perhaps justifies this gathering of odds and ends. It contains the answer Calvino gives to a journalist who asks him that tritest of questions: Who are your favourite novelists and why?'
For a moment, Calvino stops being the profound and erudite intellectual, the man engaged with the deepest, most insolvable problems of the literary act, and answers simply, with the words of a passionate reader: 'I love Stendhal above all because only in him are individual moral tension, historical tension, life force

a single thing, a linear novelistic tension. I love Pushkin because he is clarity, irony, and seriousness. I love Hemingway because he is matter-of-fact, understated, will to happiness, sadness. I love Stevenson because he seems to fly. I love Chekhov because he doesn't go farther than where he's going. I love Conrad because he navigates the abyss and doesn't sink into it. I love Tolstoy because at times I seem to be about to understand how he does it and then I don't. I love Manzoni because until a little while ago I hated him. I love Chesterton because he wanted to be the Catholic Voltaire and I wanted to be the Communist Chesterton. I love Flaubert because after him it's unthinkable to do what he did. I love the Poe of "The Gold Bug." I love the Twain of Huckleberry Finn. I love the Kipling of The Jungle Books. I love Nievo because I've reread him many times with as much pleasure as the first time, I love Jane Austen because I never read her but I'm glad she exists. I love Gogol because he distorts with clarity, meanness, and moderation. I love Dostoyevsky because he distorts with consistency, fury, and lack of moderation. I love Balzac because he's a visionary. I love Kafka because he's a realist. I love Maupassant because he's superficial. I love Mansfield because she's intelligent. I love Fitzgerald because he's unsatisfied. I love Radiguet because we'll never be young again. I love Svevo because we have to grow old.

I was ashamed of myself when I realised that life was a costume party, but I had attended with my real face.
Kafka

The danger is that if we invest too much in developing AI and too little in developing human consciousness, the very sophisticated artificial intelligence of computers might only serve to empower the natural stupidity of humans.
Yuval Noah Harari

A synonym is a word you use when you can't spell the word you first thought of.
Burt Bacharach.

As much as pooh missed piglet
He did enjoy the bacon sandwich

As it is the characteristic of great wits to say much in few words, so small wits seem to have the gift of speaking much and saying nothing.
de La Rochefoucauld

Before you diagnose yourself with depression or low self-esteem, first make sure that you are not, in fact, just surrounded by assholes.
Sigmund Freud.

Breakthrough negotiation is the art of letting the other person have your way.
William Ury

Democracy is the pathetic belief in the collective wisdom of individual ignorance.
HL Menken

Middle age is when you've met so many people that every new person you meet reminds you of someone else.
Ogden Nash

Christianity has not been tried and found wanting; it has been found difficult and not tried.
GK Chesterton

It was one of those March days when the Sun shines hot and the wind blows cold: when it is summer in the light and winter in the shade.
Dickens: Great Expectations

Art has within it that thing that you didn't know you needed.
Nick Cave

Every day above ground is a good day.
Al Pacino in Scarface

Diplomacy is the art of building ladders for others to climb down.
Bismarck

Emmanuel Kant, who grew out of the Enlightenment and who was a great believer in constitutional and democratic government, wrote an essay on war in which he had said, "The world is organically going to be driven towards some kind of consolidation." But the open question was whether it would get there by human insight or by catastrophes of a magnitude that permitted no other solution. Well, we are not on the first road. We are not on the road of human insight at the moment.
Henry Kissinger

There's an old saying: Whenever the Fed hits the brakes, someone goes through the windshield. You just never know who it's going to be.
Michael Feroli, chief economist at J.P. Morgan

If you are lonely when you are alone, then you are in bad company.
Jean Paul Sartre

I always feel it's not wise to violate rules until you know how to observe them.
T.S. Eliot

Although not in the dictionary, it is reported that "Lexophile" describes a person who loves sentences such as, "You can tune a piano, but you can't tuna fish," or, "To write with a broken pencil is pointless."
An annual competition is held by the New York Times. These are from this year's submissions:

I changed my iPod's name to Titanic. It's syncing now.

England has no kidney bank, but it does have a Liverpool.

French pancakes give me the crepes.

This girl today said she recognized me from the Vegetarians Club, but I'd swear I've never met herbivore.

I know a guy who's addicted to drinking brake fluid, but he says he can stop any time.

A thief who stole a calendar got twelve months.

When the smog lifts in Los Angeles, U.C.L.A.

A dentist and a manicurist married. They fought tooth and nail.

A will is a dead giveaway.

With her marriage, she got a new name and a dress.

Police were summoned to a day care centre where a three-year-old was resisting a rest.

A bicycle can't stand alone; it's just two tired.

The guy who fell onto an upholstery machine last week is now fully recovered.

He had a photographic memory, but it was never fully developed.

When she saw her first strands of gray hair she thought she'd dye.

Acupuncture is a jab well done. That's the point of it.

I didn't like my beard at first. Then it grew on me.

Did you hear about the crossed-eyed teacher who lost her job because she couldn't control her pupils?

When you get a bladder infection, urine trouble.

When chemists die, they barium.

I stayed up all night to see where the sun went, and then it dawned on me.

I'm reading a book about anti-gravity. I just can't put it down.

The present life of man upon earth seems to me in comparison with that time which is unknown to us like the swift flight of a sparrow through the mead-hall where you sit at supper in winter, with your Ealdormen and thanes, while the fire blazes in the midst and the hall is warmed, but the wintry storms of rain or snow are raging abroad. The sparrow, flying in at one door and immediately out at another, whilst he is within, is safe from the wintry tempest, but after a short space of fair weather, he immediately vanishes out of your sight, passing from winter to winter again. So this life of man appears for a little while, but of what is to follow or what went before we know nothing at all.
The Venerable Bede. Ecclesiastical History of the English People

There is parody, when you make fun of people who are smarter than you; satire, when you make fun of people who are richer than you; and burlesque, when you make fun of both while taking your clothes off.
PJ O'Rourke

When information is contextualised, it becomes knowledge. When knowledge compels convictions, it becomes wisdom. Yet the internet inundates users with the opinions of thousands, even millions, of other users, depriving them of the solitude required for sustained reflection that, historically, has led to the development of convictions. As solitude diminishes, so, too, does fortitude — not only to develop convictions but also to be faithful to them, particularly when they require the traversing of novel, and thus often lonely, roads. Only convictions — in combination with wisdom — enable people to access and explore new horizons.

   The digital world has little patience for wisdom; its values are shaped by approbation, not introspection. It inherently challenges the Enlightenment proposition that reason is the most important element of consciousness. Nullifying restrictions that historically have been imposed on human conduct by distance, time, and language, the digital world proffers that connection, in and of itself, is meaningful. As online information has exploded, we have turned to software programs to help us sort it, refine it, make assessments based on patterns, and to guide us in answering our questions.

   The introduction of AI — which completes the sentence we are texting, identifies the book or store we are seeking, and "intuits" articles and entertainment we might enjoy based on prior behavior — has often seemed more mundane than revolutionary. But as it is being applied to more elements of our lives, it is altering the role that our minds have traditionally played in shaping, ordering, and assessing our choices and actions.
Henry Kissinger and Eric Schmitt: The Age of AI

When I was a kid, I attempted to combine nitrous oxide and Oxo cubes. It made me a laughing stock.
Olaf Fallafel

The most difficult thing in the world is to know how to do a thing and to watch someone else do it wrong - without comment.
T. H. White

I murmured to Picasso that I liked his portrait of Gertrude Stein. Yes, he said, everybody says that she does not look like it but that does not make any difference; she will.
Alice Toklas

Avarice, ambition, revenge, or gallantry would break the strongest cords of our Constitution as a whale goes through a net. Our Constitution was made only for a moral and religious people. It is wholly inadequate to the government of any other.
John Adams, second president of the USA

How heritable is intelligence? Nothing like as heritable as money.
Steve Jones, geneticist

Men have less scruple in offending one who makes himself loved than one who makes himself feared; for love is held by a chain of obligation which, men being selfish, is broken whenever it serves their purpose; but fear is maintained by a dread of punishment which never fails.
Machiavelli: The Prince

My intuition is: we're toast. This is the actual end of history.
Geoffrey Hinton, the 'godfather of AI' and winner of the 2018 Turing Prize.

Remember, when you're dead, you don't know you're dead. It's only painful for others. The same applies when you're stupid.
Ricky Gervais

What a trillion dollars looks like ($100 bills)

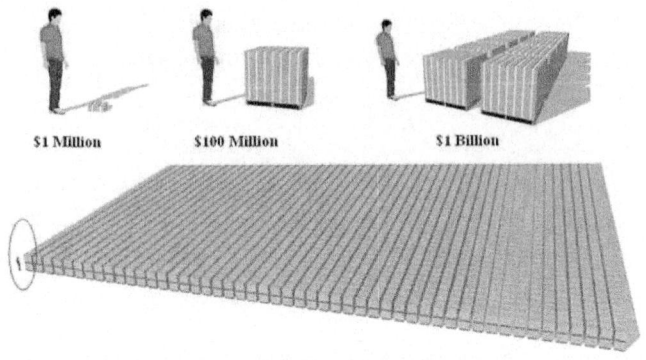

$1 Million $100 Million $1 Billion

$1 Trillion (in double-stacked pallets)

Middle age is an expensive time. One is old enough to have taste and still young enough to have appetite.
Simon Raven

I am a fully transitioned woman — all the bits and pieces you can think of have been done. Nevertheless, I would never presume to compete in female professional sports. I am a woman, but I also recognise that I went through male puberty and I think it is a matter of decency, respect and common sense to recognise that there is a difference. Although I have zero testosterone now (and for the past several years) my development as a young adult was with male testosterone. I am stronger than women who went through female puberty, although I have become less strong than men. I guess everybody has their cross to carry, so sit back, accept it and celebrate the fact that we are different.
Alexandra Leenen: letter in the Times

Your net worth to the world is usually determined by what remains after your bad habits are subtracted from your good ones.
Benjamin Franklin

The Bar-Tailed Godwit, a wading bird, migrates every year from Alaska to New Zealand - halfway round the world - without stopping. When the first one is sighted in Christchurch, they ring the cathedral bells.

The decision to "pause" exploration into AI is probably based on the 1954 short story Answer by Fredric Brown, in which scientists develop a supercalculator connecting 96 billion planets. The final switch is thrown and the machine hums into life. The chief scientist then asks the question: "Is there a God?" The answer is immediate: "Yes, now there is a God." The scientist grasps the implications and tries to turn the machine off. A bolt of lightning burns him to a crisp and fuses the switch shut.
Margaret Brown

The historian is of his own age and is bound to it by the conditions of human existence. The very words which he uses –

words like democracy, empire, war, revolution – have current connotations from which he cannot divorce them. Ancient historians have taken to using words like polis and plebs in the original, just in order to show that they have not fallen into this trap. This does not help them. They, too, live in the present, and cannot cheat themselves into the past by using unfamiliar or obsolete words, any more than they would become better Greek or Roman historians if they delivered their lectures in a chlamys or a toga. The names by which successive French historians have described the Parisian crowds which played so prominent a role in the French revolution – les sans-culottes, le peuple, la canaille, les bras-nus – are all, for those who know the rules of the game, manifestos of a political affiliation and of a particular interpretation. Yet the historian is obliged to choose: the use of language forbids him to be neutral. Nor is it a matter of words alone. Over the past hundred years the changed balance of power in Europe has reversed the attitude of British historians to Frederick the Great. The changed balance of power within the Christian churches between Catholicism and Protestantism has profoundly altered their attitude to such figures as Loyola, Luther and Cromwell. It requires only a superficial knowledge of the work of French historians of the last forty years on the French revolution to recognise how deeply it has been affected by the Russian revolution of 1917. The historian belongs not to the past but to the present.
HL Carr: What is History?

Security is mostly a superstition. It does not exist in nature. Life is either a daring adventure or nothing. Avoiding danger is no safer in the long run than outright exposure. The fearful are caught as often as the bold.
Helen Keller

Nothing will ever be attempted if all possible objections must first be overcome.
Samuel Johnson

Learn the rules like a pro so you can break them like an artist.
Picasso

To live in Australia permanently is rather like going to a party and dancing all night with your mother.
Barry Humphries

Your friend has a friend, and your friend's friend has a friend; be discreet.
The Talmud

Thinking is difficult, that's why most people judge.
Jung

Tom Whipple reports the growth in research into chat-up lines in online dating. Forty years ago, I was shown research from Berkeley University, California, showing that the most successful chat-up line to a woman was: "I like your ass." Research into the most successful line to a man remained inconclusive as they all worked.
Sheena Loveday

Only the shallow know themselves.
Oscar Wilde

He that falls in love with himself will have no rivals.
Benjamin Franklin

We did not conceive it possible that even Mr. Lincoln would produce a paper so slipshod, so loose-jointed, so puerile, not alone in literary construction, but in its ideals, its sentiments, its grasp. He has outdone himself. Has literally come out of the little end of his own horn. By the side of it, mediocrity is superb.
Chicago Times (1863) on the Gettysburg Adddress

We humans, we never really have direct access to reality. We are always cocooned by culture. We always experience reality through a cultural prism. Our political views are shaped by the stories of journalists and by the anecdotes of friends. Our sexual preferences are tweaked by movies and fairy tales. Even the way that we walk and breathe is simply nudged by cultural traditions.

Previously, this cultural cocoon was always woven by other human beings. Previous tools like printing presses, radios or televisions helped to spread the cultural ideas and creations of humans, but they could never create something new by themselves. A printing press cannot create a new book — it's always done by a human. AI is fundamentally different from printing presses, from radios from every previous invention in history, because it can create completely new ideas. It can create a new culture. And the big question is: what will it be like to experience reality through a prism produced by a non-human intelligence, by an alien intelligence?

For thousands of years, we humans basically lived inside the dreams and fantasies of other humans. We have worshipped gods, we pursued ideals of beauty, we dedicated our lives to causes that originated in the imagination of some human poet or prophet or politician. Soon, we might find ourselves living inside the dreams and fantasies of an alien artificial intelligence.
Yuval Noah Harari

A collection of employment assessments...

Since my last report, this employee has reached rockbottom and shows signs of starting to dig.

His men would follow him anywhere, but only out of morbid curiosity.

I would not allow this employee to breed.

This associate is really not so much of a has-been but more of a definitely won't be.

He would be out of his depth in a parking lot puddle.

This young lady has delusions of adequacy.

This employee should go far - and the sooner the better.

This employee is depriving a village somewhere of an idiot.

He sets low personal standards and then consistently fails to achieve them.

Everybody thinks of changing humanity and nobody thinks of changing himself.
Tolstoy

A life well spent is long.
Leonardo da Vinci

Almost every man wastes part of his life in attempts to display qualities which he does not possess, and to gain applause which he cannot keep.
Samuel Johnson

There is a great convulsion of stupidity happening in the world – mostly to do with television.
Martin Amis

An era can be said to end when its basic illusions are exhausted.
Arthur Miller

When a true genius appears in the world, you may know him by this sign, that the dunces are all in confederacy against him.
Jonathan Swift

You miss 100 percent of the shots you never take.
Wayne Gretsky

Death gives us something to do. Because it's a full-time job looking the other way.
Martin Amis

It never ceases to amaze me: we all love ourselves more than other people, but care more about their opinions than our own.
Marcus Aurelius

Pornography tells lies about women. But pornography tells the truth about men.
John Stoltenberg, anti-porn writer

Which way I fly is Hell; myself am Hell;
And, in the lowest deep, a lower deep
Still threatening to devour me opens wide,
To which the Hell I suffer seems a Heaven.
O, then, at last relent: Is there no place

Left for repentance, none for pardon left?
None left but by submission; and that word
Disdain forbids me, and my dread of shame
Among the Spirits beneath, whom I seduced
With other promises and other vaunts
Than to submit, boasting I could subdue
The Omnipotent. Ay me! they little know
How dearly I abide that boast so vain,
Under what torments inwardly I groan,
While they adore me on the throne of Hell.
With diadem and scepter high advanced,
The lower still I fall, only supreme
In misery: Such joy ambition finds.
But say I could repent, and could obtain,
By act of grace, my former state; how soon
Would highth recall high thoughts, how soon unsay
What feigned submission swore? Ease would recant
Vows made in pain, as violent and void.
For never can true reconcilement grow,
Where wounds of deadly hate have pierced so deep:
Which would but lead me to a worse relapse
And heavier fall: so should I purchase dear
Short intermission bought with double smart.
Milton: Paradise Lost

Weak people revenge. Strong people forgive. Intelligent people ignore.
Einstein

Mysteriously, there is some kind of evolutionary reality to the long and shared perception of the shags and cormorants coming from another level of creation. They are certainly among the least evolved of the seabirds, nearest in body-form and perhaps in lifestyle to the first fossil seabirds that emerged about 100 million years ago. They have not adopted the full ocean life which later-emerging birds perfected. They do not travel thousands of miles out into the riches of the ocean but stay near to shore, diving down with their giant, webbed feet to the seabed where they catch the bottom-lurking fish. Unlike the

auks or the fulmars and petrels, the shags lay many eggs, usually three, although I have seen six in a nest, white simple-looking things not the decorated beauties laid by a guillemot or an oystercatcher. They do not have the warming, featherless brood patches other birds have on the underside of their bodies, but must place the eggs on the webs of skin between their toes, shuffling into the nest when taking over from their partner. This idea is not acceptable in evolutionary terms but it is difficult not to think of the shag as a slightly Heath-Robinsonish, exotic and unrefined attempt at seabird design, as if it were an early car, full of flamboyance and inefficiency and demonstrative, set against the sleek, modern, self-containment of, say, a guillemot, which is as neat as an iPhone.
Adam Nicholson: The Seabird's Cry

Every book is the wreckage of a good idea.
Iris Murdoch

You may not be interested in war, but war is interested in you.
Leon Trotsky

There are truths which are not for all men, nor for all times.
Voltaire

While the main purpose of a door is to admit, its secondary purpose is to exclude.
Edith Wharton

Those whom the gods love do not die young; they live to be old, remaining quick to learn and feel.
Raymond Mortimer on Bernard Berenson

No one has ever had a sexual fantasy about being tied to a bed and sexually ravished by someone dressed as a liberal.
PJ O'Rourke

The opposite of addiction is not sobriety. The opposite of addiction is human connection.
Johann Hari

If you treat an individual as he is, he will remain how he is. But if you treat him as if he were what he ought to be and could be, he will become what he ought to be and could be.
Goethe

What you get free costs too much.
Jean Anouilh

There is only one way to achieve happiness on this terrestrial ball, and that is to have a clear conscience or none at all.
Dale Carnegie

What is called generosity is most often just the vanity of giving which we like more than what we give.
de La Rochefoucauld

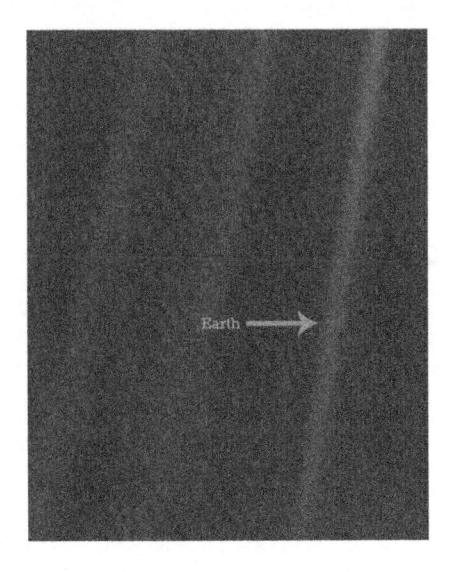

Pale Blue Dot is a photograph of earth that was taken by the Voyager 1 space probe in 1990 from a distance of about 6 billion kilometers (3.7 billion miles) as it was leaving our solar system. This is what Carl Sagan said about the photograph.

Look again at that dot. That's here. That's home. That's us. On it everyone you love, everyone you know, everyone you ever heard of, every human being who ever was, lived out their lives. The aggregate of our joy and suffering, thousands of confident religions, ideologies, and economic doctrines, every hunter and forager, every hero and coward, every creator and destroyer of civilization, every king and peasant, every young couple in love, every mother and father, hopeful child, inventor and explorer, every teacher of morals, every corrupt politician, every 'superstar' every "supreme leader' every saint and sinner in the history of our species lived there-on a mate of dust suspended in a sunbeam.

The Earth is the only world known so far to harbour life. There is nowhere else, at least in the near future, to which our species could migrate. Visit, yes. Settle, not yet. Like it or not, for the moment the Earth is where we make our stand.

It has been said that astronomy is a humbling and character-building experience. There is perhaps no better demonstration of the folly of human conceits than this distant image of our tiny world. To me, it underscores our responsibility to deal more kindly with one another, and to preserve and cherish the pale blue dot, the only home we've ever known.

Bloomberg UK Politics is listened to by people that own the country, Political Thinking is listened to by people who run the country, The Rest is Politics is produced by people who failed at running the country, Women with Balls is listened to by people who really should be running the country. And Chopper's [Politics] podcast is listened to by people who think the country should have a royal yacht. Newscast is watched by people who love the BBC, Coffee House by people who hate the BBC and The News Agents by people who also hate the BBC and used to work for it. We are blessed with a plethora of media outlets but it does get confusing.

Penny Mordant when asked what Sir Humphrey from Yes, Minister would have made of the current smorgasbord of political podcasts

> YOU TOLD ME YOU WERE INTERESTING
>
> I SAID I WAS "INTO RESTING"

The hottest places in hell are reserved for those who in times of great moral crises maintain their neutrality.
Dante

It is folly to fear what one cannot avoid.
Danish Proverb

You cannot find peace by avoiding life.
Virginia Woolf

Scandal is gossip made tedious by morality.
Oscar Wilde

During the age of sail, when wind-powered vessels were the only bridge across the vast oceans, nautical language was so pervasive that it was adopted by those on terra firma. To "toe the line" derives from when boys on a ship were forced to stand still for inspection with their toes on a deck seam. To "pipe down" was the boatswain's whistle for everyone to be quiet at night, and "piping hot" was his call for meals. A "scuttlebutt" was a water cask around which the seamen gossiped while

waiting for their rations. A ship was "three sheets to the wind" when the lines to the sails broke and the vessel pitched drunkenly out of control. To "turn a blind eye" became a popular expression after Vice-Admiral Nelson deliberately placed his telescope against his blind eye to ignore his superior's signal flag to retreat.
David Grann: The Wager

He was like a cock who thought the sun had risen to hear him crow.
George Eliot

The textbook perspective on smell is also a Western one, based on cultures where smell has long been undervalued. Plato and Aristotle argued that olfaction was too vague and ill-formed to produce anything other than emotional impressions. Darwin deemed it to be "of extremely slight service." Kant said that "smell does not allow itself to be described, but only compared through similarity with another sense."The English language confirms his view with just three dedicated smell words: stinky, fragrant, and musty. Everything else is a synonym (aromatic, foul), a very loose metaphor (decadent, unctuous), a loan from another sense (sweet, spicy), or the name of a source (rose, lemon). Of the five Aristotelian senses, four have vast and specific lexicons. Smell, as Diane Ackerman wrote, "is the one without words."
Ed Yong: An Immense World

What the world needs is more geniuses with humility, there are so few of us left.
Oscar Levant

My intuition is: we're toast. This is the actual end of history.
Geoffrey Hinton, the 'godfather of AI' and winner of the 2018 Turing Prize.

In the current climate of fierce moral certainty about the past, it sometimes feels as if we are not interested in understanding

history from the perspective of those who lived inside it. For me this is not only a crime against history but also an undermining of the defining imaginative power of fiction: to take readers into the realities of other people, whether heroes or villains, so that while we may finally judge them, we also understand how their behaviour and values grew out of the moral and cultural soil of the age in which they lived.
Sarah Dunant

Oil kindles extraordinary emotions and hopes, since oil is above all a great temptation. It is the temptation of ease, wealth, strength, fortune, power. It is a filthy, foul-smelling liquid that squirts obligingly up into the air and falls back to earth as a rustling shower of money. To discover and possess the source of oil is to feel as if, after wandering long underground, you have suddenly stumbled upon royal treasure. Not only do you become rich, but you are also visited by the mystical conviction that some higher power has looked upon you with the eye of grace and magnanimously elevated you above others, electing you its favorite.

Many photographs preserve the moment when the first oil spurts from the well: people jumping for joy, falling into each other's arms, weeping. Oil creates the illusion of a completely changed life, life without work, life for free. Oil is a resource that anesthetizes thought, blurs vision, corrupts. People from poor countries go around thinking: God, if only we had oil! The concept of oil expresses perfectly the eternal human dream of wealth achieved through lucky accident, through a kiss of fortune and not by sweat, anguish, hard work. In this sense oil is a fairy tale and, like every fairy tale, a bit of a lie. Oil fills us with such arrogance that we begin believing we can easily overcome such unyielding obstacles as time.

With oil, the last Shah used to say, I will create a second America in a generation! He never created it. Oil, though powerful, has its defects. It does not replace thinking or wisdom. For rulers, one of its most alluring qualities is that it strengthens authority. Oil produces great profits without putting a lot of people to work. Oil causes few social problems because it creates neither a numerous proletariat nor a sizable

bourgeoisie. Thus the government, freed from the need of splitting the profits with anyone, can dispose of them according to its own ideas and desires. Look at the ministers from oil countries, how high they hold their heads, what a sense of power they have, they, the lords of energy, who decide whether we will be driving cars tomorrow or walking. And oil's relation to the mosque? What vigour, glory, and significance this new wealth has given to its religion, Islam, which is enjoying a period of accelerated expansion and attracting new crowds of the faithful.
Ryszard Kapuscinski: Shah of Shahs

The tragedy of loss is not that we grieve, but that we cease to grieve, and then perhaps the dead are dead at last.
PD James: Original Sin

There is no sadder sight than a young pessimist.
Mark Twain

British people are extremely fond of the titled ass, the seeming idiot, who drawls and wears a monocle, but is always to the fore in moments of danger.
George Orwell

Jokes from the Edinburgh festival:

I have an unconscious bias. I'm biased firmly towards being unconscious
Lena Navajo

Cats are like strippers – they sit on your lap and make you think they love you.
Sikisa

Everyone says your 20s are all about finding yourself. If that's true, your 30s are about wishing you'd found somebody else.
Ginny Hogan

My relationship with my mum is like the evolution of payment technology – we went from physical contact to electronic only, then it was contactless.
Kuan-Wen Huang

Nationwide must have looked pretty silly when they opened their first branch.
William Stone

I used to be a narcissist but look at me now!
John Tothill

Women who have quarrelled with society at thirty have been glad to make up the quarrel at forty. The first wrinkle sends the penitent to confessional.
Edith Wharton

Whatever you do, always give 100%. Unless you are donating blood.
Bill Murray

A work of art does not answer questions, it provokes them.
Leonard Bernstein

We should be careful
Of each other, we should be kind
While there is still time
Philip Larkin

The problem with politics is not whether your politicians are honest or not; the problem is when politicians who tell you the truth are considered the politicians that are dishonest, and the politicians who tell you what you want to hear, they're the people who are the plain-speakers. So with the 2016 Brexit referendum... if you'd said to people at that time: Cameron and Osborne versus Boris Johnson and Nigel Farage - who are the honest people?' I bet you a large part of the population would say: "Cameron and Osborne, yeah, they're just typical

politicians; Farage and Johnson, now, they're telling it like it is."
Tony Blair in the New Statesman

 As soon as I get the idea that I understand someone, I feel it is a good corrective to remind myself that I probably don't.
Hilary Mantel

I find television very educating. Every time somebody turns on the set, I go into the other room and read a book.
Groucho Marx

There was a knock on our dressing room door. Our manager shouted, 'Keith! Ron! The Police are here!' Oh, man, we panicked and flushed everything down the toilet. Then the door opened and it was Stewart Copeland and Sting.
Keith Richards

The only known cure for presidential ambition is embalming fluid.
John McCain

As a child, I thought I hated everybody, but when I grew up, I realised it was just children I didn't like.
Philip Larkin

What you see and what you hear depends a great deal on where you are standing. It also depends on what sort of person you are.
CS Lewis: The Magician's Nephew

When wireless is perfectly applied the whole earth will be converted into a huge brain, which in fact it is, all things being particles of a real and rhythmic whole. We shall be able to communicate with one another instantly, irrespective of distance. Not only this, but through television and telephony we shall see and hear one another as perfectly as though we were face to face, despite intervening distances of thousands of

miles, and the instruments through which we shall be able to do all of this, will fit in our vest pockets.
Nikola Tesla, 1926

People are never so completely and enthusiastically evil as when they act out of religious conviction.
Umberto Eco

The fundamentalist believes that we believe in nothing. In his world view, he has his absolute certainties, while we are sunk in sybaritic indulgences. To prove him wrong, we must first know that he is wrong.
Salman Rushdie

Apricity: noun. The warmth of the sun on your back on a winter's day

War does not resolve who is right, only who is left.
Bertrand Russell

This is from Ecclesiastes 1- and was read at Nigel Lawson's memorial service. An interesting choice.

1 The words of the Teacher, son of David, king in Jerusalem:

2
"Meaningless! Meaningless!"
   says the Teacher.
"Utterly meaningless!
   Everything is meaningless."
3
What do people gain from all their labors
   at which they toil under the sun?
4
Generations come and generations go,
   but the earth remains forever.
5
The sun rises and the sun sets,
   and hurries back to where it rises.

6
The wind blows to the south
   and turns to the north;
round and round it goes,
   ever returning on its course.
7
All streams flow into the sea,
   yet the sea is never full.
To the place the streams come from,
   there they return again.
8
All things are wearisome,
   more than one can say.
The eye never has enough of seeing,
   nor the ear its fill of hearing.
9
What has been will be again,
   what has been done will be done again;
   there is nothing new under the sun.
10
Is there anything of which one can say,
   "Look! This is something new"?
It was here already, long ago;
   it was here before our time.
11
No one remembers the former generations,
   and even those yet to come
will not be remembered
   by those who follow them.

But the fact is that the world feels very dangerous at the moment. Very horrible. And in every Jewish family — every single one, mark you — there rumble tales of the prescient recent ancestor who had the sense to get out of wherever they were before it was too late, which is why we are all here, today. There are no good stories about the ones who said, "meh, it's all being overblown, that could never happen in
Lodz, Kiev, Paris, Salonika".

In my case, it was a great-grandfather from Poland and two grandparents from Czechoslovakia without whose bravery, organisation and foresight my little miscegenated crew would not have been walking around the Hampstead ponds at all. And that doesn't get forgotten in families. My mother was a doctor not because she was madly interested in medicine but because her father insisted she train for a portable profession, so that should she be forced to leave London in a hurry, she could earn a living (and get a visa) wherever she went. And that kind of attitude gets passed down.

It's why, I think, if you want to get eugenic about it, modern Jews are so very, shall we say, "visible" (one hesitates to say "successful"). Because the ones who got out of the Old Country were those who could read, speak modern languages, had real skills and, crucially, the energy to get up and go. The inward-looking, Yiddish-speaking schmendricks of the Steppe, who preferred to sit by the cholent pot, davening over back-to-front books and taking their chances with the Cossacks, they kind of got weeded out of the gene pool.
Giles Coren

Assisted dying shortens death, not life.
Rabbi Jonathan Romain

Fundamentalists lack that most civilising of human virtues: doubt.
Matthew Syed

Never have a meeting on Wednesday, as it ruins both weekends.
Jeremy Clarkson

Printed in Great Britain
by Amazon